GENESIS 34-50

THEOLOGY OF WORK PROJECT

GENESIS
34-50

THE BIBLE AND YOUR WORK
Study Series

HENDRICKSON
PUBLISHERS

Theology of Work
The Bible and Your Work Study Series: Genesis 34–50

© 2016 by Hendrickson Publishers Marketing, LLC
P.O. Box 3473
Peabody, Massachusetts 01961-3473
www.hendrickson.com

ISBN 978-1-61970-809-9

Adapted from the Theology of Work Bible Commentary, copyright © 2014 by the Theology of Work Project, Inc. All rights reserved.

All Scripture quotations, unless otherwise indicated, are taken from the Holy Bible, English Standard Version (ESV®), copyright © 2001, by Crossway, a publishing ministry of Good News Publishers. Used by permission. All rights reserved.

William Messenger, Executive Editor, Theology of Work Project
Sean McDonough, Biblical Editor, Theology of Work Project
Patricia Anders, Editorial Director, Hendrickson Publishers

Contributors:
Christopher Gilbert, "Genesis 34–50" Bible Study
Bob Stallman, "Genesis 12–50 and Work" in the Theology of Work Bible Commentary

The Theology of Work Project is an independent, international organization dedicated to researching, writing, and distributing materials with a biblical perspective on work. The Project's primary mission is to produce resources covering every book of the Bible plus major topics in today's workplaces. Wherever possible, the Project collaborates with other faith-and-work organizations, churches, universities and seminaries to help equip people for meaningful, productive work of every kind.

Printed in the United States of America

First Printing — September 2016

Contents

The Theology of Work   vii

1. Joseph Sold into Slavery in Egypt (Genesis 37:2–39:20)
    Lesson #1: Hubris and Sibling Revenge   1
    Lesson #2: Harassed Sexually and Imprisoned   5
    Lesson #3: Managing Harassment and Our Sexuality   8

2. Overcoming Evil with Godly Endurance (Genesis 39:20–41:45)
    Lesson #1: Favored and Blessing Others   12
    Lesson #2: Taking Risks for Others   16

3. Managing High Office in the World (Genesis 41:1–47:26)
    Lesson #1: Becoming Prime Minister   18
    Lesson #2: Dealing with Fame and Fortune   21
    Lesson #3: Managing a Food Crisis   24

4. Managing High Office over Family (Genesis 41:46–47:26)
    Lesson #1: Caring for the Poor   28
    Lesson #2: Applications from Joseph's Leadership   32
    Lesson #3: Dealing with Family   36

5. The Enlargement of Blessing (Genesis 44:1–50:26)
    Lesson #1: Shrewdness in Reconciling   41
    Lesson #2: The Outcome of Reconciling Leadership   44
    Lesson #3: The Family Relocates to Egypt   47

6. God Meant It for Good (Genesis 50:15–21)
    Lesson #1: God's Bigger Picture—What We Do   51
    Lesson #2: God's Bigger Picture—How We Do It   55
    Lesson #3: Joseph as a Type of Messiah   59
    Conclusion: Genesis 12:1–50:21   63

Key Verses and Themes   65

Wisdom for Using This Study in the Workplace   71

Leader's Guide   73

Chapter 1

Joseph Sold into Slavery in Egypt

(Genesis 37:2–39:20)

Lesson #1: Hubris and Sibling Revenge (37:2–36)

This Bible study on Genesis picks up where previous studies in the Theology of Work series leave off. Our first study, Genesis 1–11, deals with God's creation of the universe, and then traces humanity from the couple in the Garden of Eden to three sons of Noah and their families who spread out into the world. It ends in human failure, with the attempt "to make a name for ourselves" by constructing a city, Babel, to gather and govern the world's population. The result is judgment from God, ending in defeat, confusion, and scattering.

Our second study, Genesis 12–34, opens with God's call to a particular man, Abraham, and his wife Sarah. The work life of the first three generations is very much about family and semi-nomadic pursuits. The focus is parochial in the land of Canaan and within the clan descending from Abraham and Sarah. But, with Jacob's son Joseph, the scope of work becomes global, oriented to all peoples. Therefore, for the purposes of our study series we have created part 3 of Genesis, chapters 34–50, recounting Joseph's story from slave to prime minister in the kingdom of Egypt.

 *Food for Thought*

While the life of rural nomads might be a little removed from the settings in which most of us work, what experiences of Abraham, Isaac, or Jacob in their relationships to God and concerning their work impress you most? What can you learn from their experiences to apply to your own relationship with God in your own work?

_____

_____

_____

_____

_____

_____

_____

_____

We enter the story of Joseph to find ourselves thrust beyond the parochial life of a nomadic family to an encounter with wealthy, powerful people and their economy, justice, and government in the capital city of a dominant kingdom—which has broad relevance to the urbanized world we inhabit today.

As described in Genesis 12:2–3, God's call to Abraham came with core promises—especially the fourth promise that Abraham would be a blessing to the whole world "and in you all the families of the earth shall be blessed."

In Joseph, God directly fulfilled this promise. Indeed, Joseph sustained people from "all the world" by the system of food distribution he administered (41:57). He understood this mission to bless the world and articulated God's purpose for his life as "the saving of many lives" (50:20 NIV).

 Food for Thought

In anticipation of this study, consider your own work and name a category of work to which it belongs: for example, the building industry, agricultural science, human health services, education, and so on. What blessing can your job bestow when practiced well?

_____

_____

_____

_____

_____

_____

_____

From a young age, Joseph believed God had destined him for greatness. By means of dreams, God showed Joseph that he would rise to a position of leadership over his parents and brothers (37:5–11). For Joseph, these dreams were evidence of God's blessing promised to Abraham, and he freely divulged them. But to his brothers, the dreams were further manifestations of inordinate privilege that Joseph enjoyed as the favored son of their father, Jacob (37:3–4). Since he divulged his dreams without considering how his father's preferential treatment affected his brothers, it seems Joseph was not self-aware. Mature leaders will study their context, and by careful persuasion foster unity of purpose. Joseph's immaturity put him at great risk of payback from his brothers.

At first they plotted murder against him but settled for selling him into slavery to a caravan of traders traveling to Egypt. The merchants, in turn, sold Joseph to Potiphar, "the captain of the guard" who was "an officer of Pharaoh" in Egypt (37:36; 39:1).

 Food for Thought

A tactic used by unscrupulous managers is to find ways to remove challengers for their position. For example, a position held by a potential challenger may be eliminated "for budgetary reasons." Have you ever been removed or excluded from a job opportunity unfairly? What was it like?

_____

_____

_____

_____

_____

_____

_____

Prayer

Pause for a few moments of silence to reflect on this lesson. Then offer a prayer, either spontaneous or by using the following:

> Lord,
>
> We accept the challenge of this study to be instruments of your promise to bless all the world through Abraham's descendants, including us, his descendants by faith in Jesus. Please assist us to understand the blessing you intend for others through our work, even by injustices we might suffer, because of our salvation by "the seed of Abraham," our Lord Jesus Christ, who suffered, died, and rose for us.
>
> Amen.

Lesson #2: Harassed Sexually and Imprisoned (39:1–20)

At first, Joseph was merely "in" his master's house. Gradually, Potiphar recognized Joseph's general competence, and he promoted him to be his personal steward and "put him in charge of all that he had" (39:4).

But Potiphar's wife became interested in Joseph sexually, and she was relentless (39:7). Joseph refused her advances with notable decorum. He reminded the woman of the broad trust Potiphar had placed in him and described the relationship she sought in moral/religious terms: "wickedness" and "sin" (39:9). It seems clear he was repulsed at the thought of harming his relationships with his master and his household, as well as with God. With each demand from her, he repeated his words, until he was driven to avoid her presence. On the day she stripped him of his "garment" with no one in the house to witness, Joseph made the choice to leave the garment behind and flee naked rather than submit to her.

 *Food for Thought*

How common do you think unwanted sexual advances may be in the workplace? It might be interesting to compare your answer with others in your group. How much difference does it make if the unwanted advance comes from someone in a position of higher power, as Potiphar's wife was? Potiphar's wife created a situation common in cases of sexual exploitation—if you don't go along secretly, I'll make it look like you are guilty of a sexual offense. Could this happen in your workplace? Are there safeguards in place to prevent it?

___

The power and privilege of Potiphar's wife disadvantaged Joseph. She may well have believed that she had the right and power to use Joseph, a slave, to satisfy her sexually, yet he made it clear to her how repugnant that was to him, and how harmful to her husband.

Joseph's work required him to be at home where she was, yet he could not safely call the matter to Potiphar's attention. It was a no-win situation in which he could only lose his position, his reputation, and perhaps his life. So he chose to suffer arrest on false charges where it seems, as a slave, he had no recourse to legal assistance.

Food for Thought

It's much more frequent for the sexes in this kind of scenario to be the opposite from Joseph and Potiphar's wife—that is, for a male person in a position of power to try to take sexual advantage of a female in a less-powerful position, or of a much younger person. What does it mean that the Bible tells a story of a male victim and a female abuser? Confronted with a choice between being falsely exposed and secretly going along with the abuse, he chose the former. Why? Was it a wise choice? Would the Bible argue for all God's people to do the same thing, even at the risk of their lives?

_____

_____

_____

_____

_____

Prayer

Pause for a few moments of silence to reflect on this lesson. Then offer a prayer, either spontaneous or by using the following:

Lord,

We are grateful that you provide everything for our lives and our health in the Scriptures, including clarity about the destructive power of sexual exploitation. Help us create conditions for safety when people in power would attempt to exploit us or others sexually. Give us strength to bless others by speaking up against abusers.

Amen.

Lesson #3: Managing Harassment and Our Sexuality (39:1–20)

Sexual harassment in the workplace is a perennial problem. Whenever one person's behavior toward another is unwelcome sexually, that's harassment. People in power can and sometimes do harass others simply because they hold the upper hand.

For Jennifer, it began with her male boss leaning over the back of her chair while she pointed out on her computer screen some issues she had found in a monthly report. His hand rested on her shoulder. She felt there was nothing in this action at the moment. But as she thought about it afterwards, she remembered how he had been complimentary about her dress choices for some weeks. He was twenty-eight years her senior.

In a team photo opportunity a little while later, the same man put his arm around her shoulders and the woman on his other side. It created uncertainty in her. It was nice—affirming, even—but it was an unsolicited and unwelcome embrace.

 Food for Thought

Consider Jennifer's internal response to this situation. What would you suggest to her as a strategy for dealing with it? Is there anything in what we have seen of Joseph's story so far that might point the way?

While workers are often told to report incidents of harassment to their superiors, they know it's not necessarily safe for them to do because of the risk of obfuscation and retaliation. We can't help but notice in our news media how frequently people who report abuse are not taken seriously, and how often they suffer while the abuser gets away with it.

When Jennifer's annual review was approaching, her boss invited her to lunch to talk through any concerns she might have about her work. During lunch he praised her intellectual contribution to her team project. When she revealed some anxiety at a point in the conversation, he looked deeply into her eyes and took the opportunity to reach over and rest his hand on her leg just above the knee, reassuring her that she was regarded as a high performer for the firm.

 Food for Thought

If Jennifer was to now make a complaint about his behavior, what do you think might be the outcome? How would you advise her if this was a situation in your workplace? Why? Does the story of Joseph offer any hope or practical ideas?

_____

_____

_____

_____

_____

_____

Joseph's godliness did not rescue him from false accusation and imprisonment. If we find ourselves in a parallel situation, our godliness is no guarantee we will escape unscathed.

One Thursday evening, as Jennifer was working late, her boss snuck up from behind and kissed her on the neck with a request to come away with him for the weekend. She reproved him and refused the invitation, explaining why his advances were unwelcome. This seemed only to provoke a lewd streak in him, and he began to make suggestive gestures and invitations each time their paths crossed.

The next day, she visited the human resources office to speak with the person in charge. Since the boss was not listening to her direct communication, she was advised to make a formal complaint in writing.

This appeared to have the desired affect: the advances from her boss ceased. But, with subtlety and in informal settings with other staff, he spoke of Jennifer as "coming on" to him relentlessly and how troubling that was. He gave her a scathing performance review, and her colleagues feared for their own careers. Made to feel like a pariah in her team, she felt she had no option but to resign, and some months later did so. It took her more than a year to regain employment in her field, and she had to begin from a more junior position in another city.

The experience of Joseph and Jennifer, almost four thousand years apart, is a realistic recognition that standing up to sexual harassment in the workplace may have devastating consequences. Yet in Joseph's story, we and Jennifer can find hope that by God's grace, his plans for our permanent good will be fulfilled.

Food for Thought

If you have ever been sexually harassed at work, how did you handle its aftermath? How would you handle it now, in light of Joseph's story? And if this is something you have not experienced, what might you do to protect yourself?

_____

_____

_____

_____

_____

_____

_____

Prayer

Pause for a few moments of silence to reflect on this lesson. Then offer a prayer, either spontaneous or by using the following:

> *Lord,*
>
> *Protect us from people who would take advantage of us sexually. We have to acknowledge that, like Joseph, we may be subject to sexual harassment and face agonizingly difficult choices. Show us how to be aware of conditions in our workplaces and to bless others if we can, by making them safer. Give us the grace and courage to be truly helpful to people who experience sexual harassment.*
>
> *Amen.*

Chapter 2

Overcoming Evil with Godly Endurance

(Genesis 39:20–41:45)

Lesson #1: Favored and Blessing Others (39:20–40:23)

At this point in his life, Joseph demonstrated that he knew he was made to serve others with his talent for honest and reliable administration. Soon enough, he would realize his gift for making sense of God's guidance through dreams. He didn't allow prison to be a reason to give up on serving others in the roles for which he was made. We can see in the text that Joseph's work in prison was indeed marked by the Lord's presence, the jailer's favor, and his promotion to leadership even in the prison (39:21–23).

In a 2015 commencement address to Dartmouth students, David Brooks drew a distinction between choosing a career and being drawn by a vocation:

> People with vocations don't ask: What do I want from life? They ask: What is life demanding me to do? What gap is there in my specific circumstances around me that demands my skill set? It's not found by looking inside you for your passion. People have studied this. Eighty percent of you don't have a passion. It's found by looking outward, by being sensitive to a void and need, and then answering the chance to be of use.

 *Food for Thought*

How well do you think David Brooks interprets what is happening here for Joseph? How does this play out for you?

_____

_____

_____

_____

_____

_____

_____

In prison, Joseph found himself with two of Pharaoh's officials: the chief cupbearer and the chief baker. Many Egyptian texts mention the role of cupbearers, who not only tasted wine for quality and to detect poison, but they also enjoyed proximity to those with political power. They often became confidants who were valued for their counsel (see Neh. 2:1–4).

Chief bakers were also trusted officials who had open access to the highest persons in the land, and who may have performed other duties as high stewards of their institutions. In prison as an agent of the jailer, Joseph did the work of serving a cupbearer and a baker with their daily needs. Because he was so closely engaged with them, he was in a position to offer interpretations of their troubling dreams.

 *Food for Thought*

Being close to and serving high officials has pragmatic risks and rewards. What do you think these risks and rewards may have been in Joseph's mind? What clue in the text suggests he was not simply pragmatic in serving these men, but mindful of God's purpose in his present circumstance?

_____

_____

_____

_____

_____

_____

_____

Interpreting dreams in the ancient world was a sophisticated profession involving technical "dream books" that listed elements of dreams and their meanings. Records of the veracity of past dreams and their interpretations provided empirical evidence to support the interpreter's predictions. Joseph, however, was not schooled in this tradition and credited God with providing the interpretations that eventually proved true (40:8). In this case, the cupbearer was restored to his former post, where he promptly forgot about Joseph. The baker was hanged, and so all hope for a change in Joseph's circumstance seemed to depend on the cupbearer's goodwill.

Food for Thought

If you were Joseph, and the days became months, and the months became years with no word from the cupbearer, how would you feel? Yet Joseph must have dealt with those feelings. What history with God might he have recalled to find hope in his situation? What history with God do you recall that encourages you in seasons of disappointment?

_____

_____

_____

_____

_____

Prayer

Pause for a few moments of silence to reflect on this lesson. Then offer a prayer, either spontaneous or by using the following:

Lord,

We have hopes and aspirations for our work but often face severe setbacks. Yet each of us has a history with you as an outcome of us trusting you to remember us and work for our good. We have found you to be always true to your word, and always concerned to guard us in all circumstances. Help us to hold on to your great promise to be with each of us until the end of the age.

Amen.

Lesson #2: Taking Risks for Others (40:1–41:45)

Investing ourselves in others has risks, just as it did with Joseph's investment in the cupbearer and the baker. We can't know if a benefit will accrue to us or our organization. We may wonder about the character and motives of the people we help. Such situations are varied and complex. But they call for prayer, discernment, and action nonetheless.

The Apostle Paul wrote, "Whenever we have an opportunity, let us work for the good of all" (Gal. 6:10). If we start with an ultimate commitment to work for God, then it is easier to proceed, believing that "in all things God works for the good of those who love him, who have been called according to his purpose" (Rom. 8:28 NIV).

Joseph gained his release from the misery of "the pit" two years after the cupbearer was released. Pharaoh had some disturbing dreams, and the chief cupbearer remembered the skill of the young Hebrew in prison. The dreams about cows and stalks of grain befuddled Pharaoh's best counselors.

Joseph testified to God's ability to provide interpretations and his own role as merely the mediator of this revelation (41:16). It's worth noting that in talking with Pharaoh, Joseph did not use the covenant name of God exclusive to his own people. Instead, he consistently referred to God with the generic term of *elohim*. In this way, Joseph dignified the Egyptian king and his court, so that Pharaoh felt free to credit God with revealing to Joseph the meaning of the dreams (41:39). The testimony was received and believed.

 *Food for Thought*

How freeing is it to do what is good and right for God, despite any suspicions we might have that we're really doing any good? What effect would this attitude have on your morale in your workplace? What cultural sensitivities exist in your workplace that you need to respect in speaking of your relationship to God?

_____

_____

_____

_____

_____

_____

Prayer

Pause for a few moments of silence to reflect on this lesson. Then offer a prayer, either spontaneous or by using the following:

Lord,

How humbling it is that you know everything we cannot know about the people with whom we work. Help us not to judge them but to serve them as a service to you. Grant us faith to trust you when it seems nothing can come from our investment in fellow workers. Help us endure in the certainty that you will indeed bring your purposes to glorious completion.

Amen.

Chapter 3
Managing High Office in the World
(Genesis 41:1–47:26)

Lesson #1: Becoming Prime Minister (41:1–45)

When Joseph rightly interpreted Pharaoh's dreams, Pharaoh had such a strong sense of God's presence with Joseph that he promoted this imprisoned slave to second-in-command of Egypt! Record harvests followed by years of famine required extraordinary wisdom to prepare Egypt for survival—and in Joseph, Pharaoh saw he had the right man for the task (41:37–45).

In all this, God's word to Abraham now seemed to have a remarkable fulfillment: "I will bless those who bless you . . . and in you all the families of the earth shall be blessed" (12:3). Indeed, many nations would come to Egypt in order to feed their people during these seven years of famine.

 Food for Thought

Consider the goal of your own work: why are you doing it, and what gives you the most enjoyment? What if you were promoted so that your work could bless others in ways you had only imagined? How would you respond?

Joseph confessed his inability to meet the challenge placed before him, while finding an appropriate way to attribute success to God. In so doing, he forged a powerful defense against the pride that often accompanies public acclaim—and surely he had inducement to become proud.

Joseph's promotion brought him significant perks of office: a royal signet ring and gold chain, fine clothing appropriate to his elevated position, official transportation, a new Egyptian name, and an Egyptian wife from an upper-class family (41:41–45). In every material sense, he had made it to the top.

 Food for Thought

Promotion is sometimes a risky hurdle in the adventure of our work. It is one thing to aspire to new responsibility, and another to remain grounded and deliver the higher level of service required. When we attribute to God our position and our opportunities, how does that help us to safely manage transitions like job advancement? To what degree is your current success (or lack of it) due to God?

If ever there was a lure to leave his Hebrew heritage behind, this one had to be an extraordinary enticement to Joseph. Perhaps this was the greatest test he faced in fulfilling his part in the eternal purposes of God. Why should he care for a nomadic family who conspired to murder him and then sold him off as a slave in a foreign land—especially given that the whole of Egypt was his now?

Many people call out to God for help in failure and defeat. It is when we deal with success that it may be hardest to seek God, yet that is probably when we need God's help most. The biblical text here gives several clues to the godly way Joseph managed his promotion, and some of this had to do with his long years of preparation for this moment.

 Food for Thought

Why do you think we are more likely to be at risk in the managing of success rather than failure? What are some emotional triggers in failure as compared to success or acclaim? Explain or outline a strategy for staying in touch with God and following his ways in seasons of high achievement.

_____

_____

_____

_____

_____

_____

Prayer

Pause for a few moments of silence to reflect on this lesson. Then offer a prayer, either spontaneous or by using the following:

> Lord,
>
> *We are humbled by what we see in the story of Joseph. When he was given the highest possible position as an administrator, he stayed faithful to your people and your eternal purposes. Grant that we too might accept achievement as a way to bless the world as you intend, especially the people of God, in carrying out your eternal plans.*
>
> *Amen.*

Lesson #2: Dealing with Fame and Fortune (41:1–45)

God-given dreams of leadership convinced the young Joseph that he had a divinely ordained purpose and destiny, and he never forgot it. In this confidence, he seemed forgiving of others. There is no hint he held a grudge against the forgetful cupbearer, and when he met his jealous brothers years later, he forgave them.

So, before Pharaoh promoted him, Joseph knew that the Lord was with him. The evidence mounted in many remarkable experiences even as a slave and a prisoner, through serving others with work according to his gifts. His habit of giving God credit was not only true and therefore right, but it also reminded Joseph himself that his skills were from the Lord.

 *Food for Thought*

In your own work, what evidences of God's love and direction for you do you treasure? What personal disciplines help you remember what God has done for you, in good times and bad?

_____

_____

_____

_____

_____

_____

_____

Had Joseph been vengeful over the hardships he endured he might have languished in a prison full of embittered souls. But because he remained courteous and humble in his work, he stood out. For him it was no stretch to welcome the opportunity to do whatever he could to help Pharaoh and the Egyptian people. Even when the Egyptians were bereft of currency and livestock, Joseph earned the trust of the Egyptian people and Pharaoh (41:55). The story of his life as an administrator shows Joseph consistently devoting himself to effective management for the good of others.

Joseph's story to this point reminds us that in our broken world, God's response to our prayers doesn't necessarily come quickly. Joseph was seventeen years old when his brothers sold him into slavery (37:2). His final release from captivity came when he was thirty (41:46), thirteen long years later.

Food for Thought

What might these thirteen long years suggest in regard to your own journey? Why do you think time is an important part of our preparation for advancement? Consider what attitudes God may want to develop in you as habits to become ready, as Joseph was ready, for higher office.

_____

_____

_____

_____

_____

_____

Prayer

Pause for a few moments of silence to reflect on this lesson. Then offer a prayer, either spontaneous or by using the following:

Lord,

In a fast-paced world, we tend to forget the need for nurture and development over time in our hearts, always wanting completion now! Help us to slow down and ponder the best use of the days you provide for us at work. We want to be prepared for the best you have for us, participants in the household of faith in which "all the families of the earth shall be blessed."

Amen.

Lesson #3: Managing a Food Crisis (41:46–57; 47:13–26)

As his first act, "Joseph . . . went through all the land of Egypt" on an inspection tour (41:46). In this way, he became familiar with the people who managed agriculture, the locations and conditions of the fields, the crops, the roads, and means of transportation. He didn't expect to accomplish his task on his own. He had to establish and oversee the training of what amounted to a Department of Agriculture and Revenue.

During the seven years of abundant harvest, Joseph stored the grain in cities (41:48–49). During the seven lean years that followed, Joseph dispensed it to the Egyptians and others affected by the widespread famine. To create and administer all this, while surviving the political intrigue of an absolute monarchy, required exceptional talent.

 Food for Thought

If you were asked to take over leadership in work you have always wanted to do, what would be your first act in the new position? How would you go about raising a team to assist you? By what set of values would you want them to govern their tasks?

_____

_____

_____

_____

_____

_____

Joseph's primary concern was for the people of Egypt, rather than taking personal advantage of his new position at the head of the royal court. We see him maintaining his faith in God, giving his children names that credited God with healing his emotional pain and making him fruitful (41:51–52).

While Joseph recognized that his wisdom and discernment were gifts from God, he also knew he had much to learn about the land of Egypt and its agriculture. As the senior administrator, his work affected the whole fabric of the nation's life. In his role, he needed to understand legislation, communication, negotiation, transportation, safe and efficient methods of food storage, building, economic strategizing and forecasting, record-keeping, payroll, the handling of transactions both by means of currency and through bartering, human resources, and the acquisition of real estate.

 Food for Thought

Imagine you are a journalist investigating a leader's performance. How would you discern whether the person works for the good of constituents or clients, or cares more for the perks of office? What are some telltale signs?

_____

_____

_____

_____

_____

_____

Joseph's extraordinary abilities with respect to God and people did not operate in separate domains. The genius of Joseph's success lay in the effective integration of his God-given gifts with his acquired competencies. For Joseph, all of this was the work God gave him to do.

Pharaoh had already characterized Joseph as "discerning and wise" (41:39), characteristics that enabled Joseph to do the work of strategic planning and administration. The Hebrew words for "wise" and "wisdom," *hakham* and *hokhmah*, denote a high level of mental perceptivity. But they also describe a wide range of practical skills, including craftsmanship of wood, precious stones, and metal (Exod. 31:3–5; 35:31–33), tailoring (Exod. 28:3; 35:26, 35), as well as administration (Deut. 34:9; 2 Chron. 1:10), and legal justice (1 Kings 3:28). These skills are found among unbelievers as well, but the wise enjoy the special blessing of God, who intends for Israel to display God's ways to the nations (Deut. 4:6).

 Food for Thought

What perceptive and practical skills (biblical wisdom) are required in your field of work? What would you look for in a leader? Have you ever considered that your own work, when applied with careful thought and skill, is a God-given task by which God can bless the world?

_____

_____

_____

Prayer

Pause for a few moments of silence to reflect on this lesson. Then offer a prayer, either spontaneous or by using the following:

Lord,

How easy it is to see our day-to-day work as mundane and relatively meaningless. Thank you that from the beginning of the biblical record you make it plain that our work matters—that it is one of your great means of blessing the world. Please help us work using our utmost abilities wherever we are found as your workers.

Amen.

Chapter 4

Managing High Office over Family

(Genesis 41:46–47:26)

Lesson #1: Caring for the Poor (47:13–26)

When the famine continued to devastate Egypt, the people eventually exhausted their money supply. Prolonged lack of food could have made them desperate for themselves and for their families, resulting in lawlessness, death, and disease.

But Joseph adapted to the people's need, allowing them to barter their livestock for food. This plan served the people well for one year, during which Joseph collected horses, sheep, goats, cattle, and donkeys (47:15–17).

Some of the complexities he must have managed included determining the fair value of the animals and establishing an equitable system for exchange. Providing continued equitable food distribution was an acutely important administrative matter for the sake of the well-being of Egypt.

 Food for Thought

Consider the way your work helps people in times of economic distress. To what extent does Joseph's creativity and compassion have something to teach you or your organization? Was Joseph able to reconcile the tensions inherent in both serving the Pharaoh and helping the people at the same time?

_____

_____

_____

_____

_____

_____

_____

The plight of the people worsened. When all of the livestock had been traded, they sold their land to Pharaoh—and then sold themselves as slaves to him (47:18–21).

It was an unfolding tragedy Joseph had to witness and also allow, yet he permitted it without exploiting their powerlessness. The properties needed to be valued fairly in exchange for seed for planting (47:23). Then Joseph enacted an enduring law that people return 20 percent of the harvest to Pharaoh. So a system to monitor and enforce compliance and a revenue department were needed.

But societies are complex. When the priestly families were exempted from selling their land, because Pharaoh supplied them with a fixed allotment of food (47:22, 26), Joseph had to manage perceptions of inequitable redistribution as well.

 *Food for Thought*

Some take issue with Joseph as an official in a repressive society, saying he became part of its power structure, personally imposing slavery on uncounted numbers of people (47:21). What do you think Genesis 47 suggests he accomplished with his strategy?

_____

_____

_____

_____

_____

The resources of organizations, even governments, are finite. Joseph's strategy kept the kingdom of Egypt solvent, its economy viable, and the people alive and able to work the land they once owned while still living in their original homes. The tax on their employment was approximately the same as or less than it is today in modern nation states. Yet that also included rental of the land now owned by the state.

For administrators in crises, it often becomes a matter of choosing the lesser of two evils in caring for victims of a catastrophe. In the 2015 earthquake in Nepal, for example, administrators had to force people to live outdoors until their homes were inspected for safety. Outdoors, there was the long-term possibility of death by exposure to cold or disease. Indoors, there was the immediate probability of more quakes, and burial beneath the rubble of their homes. However we perceive he carried it out, Joseph experienced God's guidance in these difficult tasks. Consider the outcome.

Because of Joseph, the people of Egypt survived a social catastrophe. His strategy and implementation of the plan made Egypt an exporter of grain to the rest of the world during the famine (41:57). In this case, God's fulfillment of his promise that Abraham's descendants would be a blessing to the world occurred not only *for* the benefit of foreign nations, but even *through* the industry of a foreign nation, Egypt.

In fact, God's blessing for the people of Israel came only after and through his blessing of foreigners. God did not raise up an Israelite in the land of Israel to provide only for Israel's relief during the famine. Instead, God enabled Joseph, working in and through the Egyptian government, to provide for the needs of all the people, Israelite and Egyptian (47:11–12).

 Food for Thought

On careful reading of Joseph's story, we see he always had God's global perspective in mind and yet a concern for ordinary people's welfare. What do you suppose is God's overarching plan for your field of work, and how might you do more to ensure people are well served in it?

Prayer

Pause for a few moments of silence to reflect on this lesson. Then offer a prayer, either spontaneous or by using the following:

Lord,

Our broken world often requires our work to deal with human crises of poverty. Throughout Scripture, we see you called your people to care for the poor from the very beginning. As we look at our tasks today, open our hearts to perceptions of your overarching purpose so we might safely walk the tightrope between compassion and wisdom and bring blessing to many in your name.

Amen.

Lesson #2: Applications from Joseph's Leadership (41:46–57)

The major plot of the biblical story of Joseph's management of the food crisis is its effect on the family of Israel. There is, however, sufficient detail in the account of Joseph's managerial work from which we can derive some practical applications. Consider the following:

1. Gratefully and appropriately acknowledge the gifts God has given you.

2. Commit yourself to God first, and then expect him to direct and establish you in your work.

3. At the beginning of your employment, become as familiar as possible with coworkers, the conditions of their employment, and the services they provide.

4. Educate yourself about how to do your job and carry it out with excellence.

5. Pray for discernment regarding the future so you can make wise plans.

 Food for Thought

In these five points, note the interplay of a relationship with God and concern for people. How well is this pattern reflected in the ultimate goal of the business or institution in which you work? What might you be able to accomplish there if you made these five points normal behavior in your work?

_____

_____

_____

_____

_____

_____

Here are five more application points to consider:

1. Seek the practical good for others, knowing that God has placed you where you are to be a blessing.

2. Establish the norm of fairness in all your dealings, so that when the circumstances are grim and people are vulnerable they will know you won't exploit them.

3. Even though others might recognize God's presence in your life and special talents you may have, do not broadcast these in a self-serving effort to gain respect.

4. Although your exemplary service may propel you to prominence, remember your founding mission as God's servant. Your life does not consist in what you gain for yourself.

5. Value the godliness of myriad types of honorable work that society needs.

 Food for Thought

Which of the above five applications challenges you the most? What would have to change in your attitude for you to apply them wholeheartedly?

_____

_____

_____

_____

_____

_____

Lastly, here are another five applications for your work life:

1. Generously extend the fruit of your labor as widely as possible to those who truly need it, regardless of what you think of them as individuals.

2. Accept the fact that God may bring you into a particular field of work under extremely challenging conditions. This does not mean that something has gone terribly wrong or that you are out of God's will.

3. Have courage that God will fit you for the task.

4. Accept that sometimes we will need to choose the best of terrible pathway options through a crisis.

5. Believe that what you do not only will benefit those you see and meet, but also has the potential to touch lives for many generations to come. God is able to accomplish abundantly far more than we can ask or imagine (Eph. 3:20).

 Food for Thought

Which of these final five applications touches on changes you'd like to make in your work life? Write down your thoughts and then ask God for help. Look at the list again and rearrange it in an order of priority that seems right for your present circumstance.

_____

_____

_____

_____

_____

_____

_____

Prayer

Pause for a few moments of silence to reflect on this lesson. Then offer a prayer, either spontaneous or by using the following:

Lord,

Lists of "must do's" can be daunting, and this one asks much of us. We pray for your gracious help in applying to our work lives these character traits of Joseph that he also learned as he sought continual relationship with you. We come with confidence in asking this because Jesus exhorted us to ask, seek, and knock. It is in his name we pray.

Amen.

Lesson #3: Dealing with Family (42:1–43:34)

As the famine affected lands far and wide, news spread that Egypt had a supply of grain it was willing to sell. Before their own supply was exhausted, Jacob (Joseph's father) sent his sons from Canaan to Egypt in an attempt to buy food. This brought them face to face with their brother, whom they had sold as a slave and who, unbeknownst to them at the moment, was now the governor of Egypt.

Recognizing them, Joseph behaved shrewdly. From his position of power, he could discover if anything had changed in the characters of these men who had a history of deceit and violence against others. He masked his true identity with his Egyptian appearance and spoke in the language of commerce. He then accused them as spies of a foreign power (42:7, 9, 14, 16; 44:3–5).

 *Food for Thought*

To what extent do you think Joseph was acting appropriately or inappropriately in his shrewdness? Why?

_____

_____

_____

_____

_____

_____

_____

For the brothers, it was like a prosecutor who was also the judge conducting a tough interrogation. But an easygoing transparency from Joseph would not have tested their true nature. He had to be shrewd.

Shrewdness in the biblical narratives may be exercised for good or for ill. While the serpent is characterized as "the shrewdest of all the wild animals" (Gen. 3:1 NLT) and employed shrewd methods for disastrously evil purposes, the Hebrew word for shrewdness, *ormah*, is also translated as "good judgment," "prudence," "clever," and "cunning" (Prov. 12:23; 13:16; 14:8; 22:3; 27:12).

When the stakes are high in our workplaces, shrewdness is essential. Human nature gravitates toward self-serving subterfuge, manipulation, deceit, and betrayal, with a plethora of corrupt motives. With the clearest eye for human sin (Mark 7:21–23), Jesus counsels us to be "as shrewd as snakes and harmless as doves"

(Matt. 10:16 NLT). Scripture from Genesis to the New Testament commends shrewdness for noble purposes (Prov. 1:4; 8:5, 12).

 Food for Thought

In your own experience, what rewards, inducements, or even lack of reward in the nature of your work seem to prompt the basest behaviors? What "shrewd" systems are in place to maintain the integrity of product or service delivery?

_____

_____

_____

_____

_____

_____

_____

_____

Joseph's shrewdness had the intended effect of testing his brothers' integrity, for they returned the silver Joseph secretly packed in the baggage (43:20–21). When Joseph treated Benjamin more generously, they were further tested, but there was no animosity among them as there had been when they had sold Joseph into slavery.

Joseph was not taking moral high ground, as if he was closer to God than his brothers. But his long career of suffering in God's service gave him the necessary awareness of the disintegrating effect of ubiquitous human crookedness. He could see that God's promise to make Abraham into a vast nation was under serious threat. He therefore acted to reverse that scenario.

This is the mark of the godly shrewdness in Joseph: he gained nothing from his scheme for himself. Already blessed by God, his actions were solely in the service of *becoming* a blessing to others. His actions actually kept the family intact, when its trajectory was toward disintegration.

 Food for Thought

Many of us live with a sense of deficit rather than blessing. Count and pray over your blessings, even if that is already your habit. In what circumstances have you become aware of God's goodness to you? Where might this be applied in your work life in order to counter the destructive forces of ubiquitous human sin?

Prayer

Pause for a few moments of silence to reflect on this lesson. Then offer a prayer, either spontaneous or by using the following:

Lord,

Our integrity at work is tested constantly, and so is the integrity of those around us. Help us to remember the times you rescued us from our own sinfulness or the sin of others. Show us how to be a blessing in our workplaces that need constant vigilance to work with the integrity you originally intended. Teach us godly shrewdness.

Amen.

Chapter 5

The Enlargement of Blessing
(Genesis 44:1–50:26)

Lesson #1: Shrewdness in Reconciling (44:1–34)

When the brothers returned from Canaan with Benjamin, they experienced yet another prosecutorial trial. Joseph framed Benjamin for an imaginary crime and claimed Benjamin as a slave in recompense. When he demanded that the brothers return home to Jacob without Benjamin (44:17), Judah emerged as the group's spokesman.

What gave Judah the standing to take on this role? He had hatched the plan to sell his own brother as a slave (37:27) and had broken faith with his family by marrying a Canaanite (38:2), had raised such wicked sons that the Lord put two of them to death (38:7, 10), ignored justice for his son's widow, and while seeking a Canaanite prostitute, slept with his daughter-in-law, who reading his character well, sought justice through her own shrewd deception (38:24).

But Joseph now heard a deeply changed man. Judah exhibited compassion in the tale of the family's near starvation experience, of his father's love for Benjamin, and of his promise to his father that he would bring Benjamin back home, lest Jacob literally die from grief. Amazingly, Judah offered to substitute *himself* (44:33–34) in place of Benjamin!

 **Food for Thought**

If the brothers had responded true to their previous form, what might they have done in this situation? Why do you think Judah took this stance? What did it reveal about him ultimately?

_____

_____

_____

_____

_____

_____

_____

With Judah, the eminent leader, so apparently broken from his former wickedness, Joseph proceeded to bless the brothers as God intended. He disclosed to them the full truth: "I am Joseph" (45:3). Then he calmed the terrified men by pointing to the work of God, who was responsible for placing Joseph in charge of all Egypt (45:8). Theologian Bruce Waltke calls this scene an anatomy of reconciliation:

> It is about loyalty to a family member in need, even when he or she looks guilty; giving glory to God by owning up to sin and its consequences; overlooking favoritism; offering up oneself to save another; demonstrating true love by concrete acts of sacrifice that create a context of trust; discarding control and the power of knowledge in favor of intimacy; embracing deep compassion, tender feelings, sensitivity, and forgiveness; and talking to one another. A dysfunctional family that allows these virtues to embrace it will become a light to the world.

Food for Thought

Apply Bruce Waltke's list of virtues to recent work relationship conflicts you have observed or been party to, and consider how the outcome might have changed if such behaviors had been evident in the leadership.

_____

_____

_____

_____

_____

_____

_____

_____

Prayer

Pause for a few moments of silence to reflect on this lesson. Then offer a prayer, either spontaneous or by using the following:

> Lord,
>
> *It is apparent in this part of the story that you are the one who changes hearts. And, like Judah, we want to measure up to the high calling of our blessedness in your family. Please soften our hearts in our workplaces, and grant us eyes to see and hearts willing to initiate equitable, nonjudgmental, sacrificial leadership among our fellow workers.*
>
> *Amen.*

Lesson #2: The Outcome of Reconciling Leadership (44:1–34)

We might also suggest that a dysfunctional business embracing the virtues outlined by Waltke above can also become a light to the world and a great place to work. But that assertion might also be challenged by many who regard the marketplace as a naturally aggressive and necessarily competitive arena.

We know that God is more than able to bring his blessings to the world through deeply flawed people like us. Yet, as we saw in the lesson on shrewdness, leaders must operate with the attitude that "trust requires trustworthiness," and learn to discern it by testing it.

 Food for Thought

What kind of pushback would you expect in your workplace if a leader dared to introduce the principles outlined by Waltke? How would you go about dealing with that resistance? How would you earn trust in that setting?

_____

_____

_____

_____

_____

_____

From the very beginning of God's covenant to bless Abraham's family, we find that *when* repentance is real, *then* God's grace is freed for blessing. God expected leaders of Israel to take the blame for the sins of others. On the few occasions when such behavior was evident from Israel's notable leaders, it stood in stark contrast to the world around them. This would be true for us also today.

For example, when Israel sinned regarding the golden calf, Moses said to God,

> "Alas, this people has sinned a great sin; they have made for themselves gods of gold. But now, if you will only forgive their sin—but if not, blot me out of the book that you have written." (Exod. 32:31–32)

And when he saw the angel of the Lord striking down the people, David prayed,

> "What have they done? Let your hand, I pray, be against me and against my father's house." (2 Sam. 24:17)

But God never required them to make good on their offers.

Why do you think God would listen and grant the petitions of Moses and David, without taking up their self-sacrificing offers?

_____

_____

_____

_____

_____

_____

_____

Someone else in Scripture prayed for the forgiveness of the people God had given him to lead, offering himself in their place—and his willingness *was* accepted. Only Jesus, the Lion of the tribe of Judah, was required to pay that price. He offered himself for the sins of the world:

> "For this reason the Father loves me, because I lay down my life in order to take it up again. No one takes it from me, but I lay it down of my own accord." (John 10:17–18)

Disciples of the Good Shepherd are required to take up their cross and follow after their master. This can mean costly decisions in our workplaces in order to bring about genuine heartfelt repentance in others, whether colleagues or bosses.

 Food for Thought

Can you recall a moment in your work life in which leaders took the blame for mistakes made by others? If so, how did it affect the leader? How did it affect the people he led? What about the alternative scenario of blaming the workers? What is the main challenge laid out to you in this chapter of our study?

_____

_____

_____

_____

_____

_____

_____

Prayer

Pause for a few moments of silence to reflect on this lesson. Then offer a prayer, either spontaneous or by using the following:

Lord,

How difficult it is for us to accept responsibility for our own actions, let alone for the actions of those around us. Thank you that you laid down your life to free us from the burden of self-righteousness. Help us to bless our colleagues with the same willingness to lead with humility and to commit acts of grace and mercy when others' actions go wrong.

Amen.

Lesson #3: The Family Relocates to Egypt (45:16–47:12)

With Pharaoh's blessing, Joseph was lavish in helping his family relocate to Egypt, the land of plenty. Pharaoh gave Joseph's brothers "the best of all the land of Egypt" (45:20) in Goshen, supplying them for their trip home to Canaan and the transportation of the entire family back to Egypt.

> And Pharaoh said to Joseph, "Say to your brothers, '. . . I will give you the best of the land of Egypt, and you shall eat the fat of the land.' And you, Joseph, are commanded to say, '. . . Have no concern for your goods, for the best of all the land of Egypt is yours.'" (45:17–20)

Pharaoh's generosity was extraordinary. Of course, Joseph had saved Pharaoh's entire nation, yet it is easy for people to forget what others have done for them in times past, as the cupbearer had done.

 *Food for Thought*

Imagine a parallel magnanimous show of thanks occurring in your work context. What positive effects might it have? What might be the downside for recipients accepting such a grand gesture? How might it affect the relationships among the leader, the people being thanked, and the general population of your workplace?

_____

_____

_____

_____

_____

_____

_____

With the advantage of hindsight we can't help but notice there is now something wrong with this picture. God had promised Abraham and his descendants the land of *Canaan*, not Egypt. But for Joseph, Egypt was the land where God put him and it now offered safety and opportunity. He could not but feel that because he had "arrived," his family's immediate future was secure there. It's clear he didn't sense a call to lead the family back to Canaan.

Ultimately, his foresight couldn't extend to events long after his death. Indeed, the preacher in Ecclesiastes makes it clear that in the normal run of human life we just can't know such things (see Eccl. 9:1–10:17 in the study on Ecclesiastes/Song of Songs in The Bible and Your Work study series).

 Food for Thought

Considering the detour of the covenant family to a land far from Canaan, what do you make of the consequence of Joseph's and Pharaoh's benevolence? Are there forms of generosity in your field of work that might pull the work itself away from its God-designed purpose? What about inducements to you that threaten to distract you from the main purpose of your work?

_____

_____

_____

_____

_____

_____

_____

Each generation needs to remain faithful to God and receive God's blessings in their own time. Regrettably, Joseph's descendants forgot God's promises and drifted into faithlessness.

Yet God did not forget his promise to Abraham, Isaac, Jacob, and their descendants. Among their descendants God would raise up new men and women to impart God's promised blessings.

 *Food for Thought*

As we have discussed previously, success is often a greater challenge to our faithfulness than failure is. Consider whatever successes you are presently experiencing. In what ways do they change your life, your work, or your self-perception? What new forms and patterns may your faithfulness need to take?

_____

_____

_____

_____

_____

_____

_____

Prayer

Pause for a few moments of silence to reflect on this lesson. Then offer a prayer, either spontaneous or by using the following:

Lord,

How easily we are swayed into believing a significant success is a mountaintop where we can rest from continuing in your commission to restore all things. Help us to see that after us will come others who need us to continue in faithfulness and service. Grant that we always look over the horizon and help the next generation prepare for it.

Amen.

Chapter 6

God Meant It for Good

(Genesis 50:15–21)

Lesson #1: God's Bigger Picture—What We Do (50:15–21)

At the end of a long life, Joseph saw the bigger picture of God's plan and believed that God would take his people back to Canaan. Like his father, he sought a promise from the next generation that his own bones would be buried there (50:25; Heb. 11:22).

Long after Joseph died, Egypt's relationship with Israel would turn from hospitality to hostility. And Joseph's benevolence had the unintended consequence of delivering his less faithful posterity into many generations of slavery to a different Pharaoh.

As we have discovered, Joseph was a man of keen insight who planned for the future and who brought about God's blessing assigned to him. But God did not reveal to him the future rise of a "new king . . . who did not know Joseph" (Exod. 1:8).

From this we can learn that each generation must develop in its own faithfulness to God and receive God's blessings in its own time. Regrettably, Joseph's descendants largely failed to rely on God's covenant and perhaps drifted into believing it was merely a family legend. Yet God did not forget his promise to Abraham, Isaac, Jacob, and their descendants, but worked through a faithful remnant of his people to impart his promised blessings.

 *Food for Thought*

This part of the story raises issues of succession of leadership and maintenance of vision and mission in our industries. Consider how Joseph prepared his people for his own passing. What preparations can you make to help those who will succeed you in your present work?

_____

_____

_____

_____

_____

_____

_____

Joseph discovered one of the finest God-given insights of his life upon hearing the penitent words of his brothers. Indeed, it is a signal statement in the book of Genesis. "Even though you intended to do harm to me," he told them, "God intended it for good, in order to preserve a numerous people, as he is doing today. So have no fear; I myself will provide for you and your little ones" (50:20–21).

Joseph's reference to "numerous people" echoes God's covenantal promise to bless "all families of the earth" (Gen. 12:3). From our vantage point today, we can see that God sent far more blessing than Joseph could ever have asked or imagined (see Eph. 3:20).

 *Food for Thought*

Working people universally encounter hurtful personal injustices as well as recognition for achievement. In his suffering, Joseph recognized God at work, fulfilling his promises. What hurts and injustices have been done to you in your work and life? Has God turned them around and used them for good? Is there any way you can help or hinder God's goodness from flowing out of the situations that have harmed you?

_____

_____

_____

_____

_____

_____

_____

Joseph's opportunities for work as a slave, a prisoner, and the governor of Egypt had a real, practical, serious value: to preserve lives. All genuine work has the opportunity to serve people by improving their experience of mortal life.

Many Christians at work in the marketplace know that in the church there is a tendency to reduce their purpose in work to only telling others about God or building relationships so that people might want to know God. Joseph's work, indeed the entire book of Genesis, says that our commission from God is far more than this. The products we make and the services we deliver in a material world are themselves crucial to God's design for human flourishing. Sometimes we lose sight of our work as a piece of this bigger whole, and we also lose sight of the result of the work. Joseph took the larger perspective on his work—even service as a slave and in prison was an important part of God's design, even if Joseph couldn't understand how, and even if it was imposed upon him unjustly.

Consequently, he was not discouraged from diligence at his work by its inevitable ups and downs. Eventually, his trust in God's larger purpose was vindicated beyond his wildest hopes—fulfilling what God had told him back in his dreams as a seventeen-year-old.

 Food for Thought

What do you imagine is God's purpose for your field of work? What external or internal influences limit your freedom to pursue it? From Joseph's story, what might help you maintain your sense of mission in your work?

_____

_____

_____

_____

_____

_____

_____

Prayer

Pause for a few moments of silence to reflect on this lesson. Then offer a prayer, either spontaneous or by using the following:

> *Lord,*
>
> *Our lives at work are often buffeting. In difficult times, we tend to lose sight of the overarching importance of our daily tasks and easily become discouraged. Grant that we might take hold of Joseph's story in a new way to reinvigorate our sense of purpose as we participate in blessing our broken world.*
>
> *Amen.*

Lesson #2: God's Bigger Picture—How We Do It (50:15–21)

While our daily tasks are important both to God and to the people we serve, so are the relationships we develop through our work. Put another way, we can say that *what* we do and *how* we do it are two aspects of the same important purpose God has for his people at work. Not all Christians can be at the top of their fields—often unbelievers are more skilled and outrank us. But a unique contribution Christians can make, no matter where they are placed at work, is to offer the graciousness of forgiveness to their colleagues and clients.

Joseph's reassurance of his brothers is certainly a model of forgiveness. Following the instruction of his father, Joseph forgave his brothers and thus verbally released them from guilt. But his forgiveness—like all true forgiveness—was more than verbal. Despite the great cost to Joseph of his brothers' malice, he left the matter in God's hand to judge. "Am I in the place of God?" he asked them (50:19). He did not usurp God's role as judge but helped his brothers to connect with God who had saved them.

 Food for Thought

Christians are not all gifted for leadership as Joseph was. We are not all A students and high achievers. This raises the question of graciousness, especially forgiveness, as a distinctive of Christian work. What are the costs you have to count in offering forgiveness as a Christian value at work?

_____

_____

_____

_____

_____

_____

_____

Because Joseph had experienced extraordinary consolation and mercy from God, he was able to offer this consolation of God's grace and mercy. In the aftermath of this enormous blessing, Joseph used the extensive resources of Egypt, which God had placed under his control, to support them materially so that they could prosper. The relationship Joseph had with his brothers included not just their domestic family life but also their economic interests.

 *Food for Thought*

What do you think of as the blessings you have received from God, even materially? What might Joseph's use of resources suggest about how we use the resources we have in our jobs?

_____

_____

_____

_____

_____

_____

_____

Home and livelihood have been integral to families, tribes, and nations for thousands of years, and the same need for forgiveness of destructive behavior is essential at home and in workplaces.

But it is hard to offer forgiveness to people whom we believe have wronged us. It may be especially hard to do in our workplaces because we often confuse forgiveness with weakness, and we sense that weakness is a formula for failure at work.

The question, really, is whether we believe that forgiveness is indeed God's intent for our work, or whether it is just something we talk piously about at church.

 *Food for Thought*

Name an area of your work experience where you sense the lack of graciousness and mercy. What does this do to morale in your workplace? What does it ask of you as a Christian when you are faced with aggression and unjust behavior?

_____

_____

_____

_____

_____

_____

_____

Prayer

Pause for a few moments of silence to reflect on this lesson. Then offer a prayer, either spontaneous or by using the following:

> *Lord,*
>
> *It can seem that the hardest request you make of us is to forgive those who deliberately hurt us—yet the testimony of those who do forgive is one of freedom and joy. You, Lord, are the true judge. As you have released us from judgment by making it fall on your Son, empower us to offer forgiveness in all sincerity at home and at work.*
>
> *Amen.*

Lesson #3: Joseph as a Type of Messiah (37:2–50:15)

While most of our work life takes place in the public realm, and we ought to respect that others do not share our Christian faith, the division of life into separate compartments labeled "sacred" and "secular" is something foreign to the worldview of Scripture. It is not sectarian or merely "religious," then, to affirm that as Christians forgiveness is a sound workplace practice.

Joseph's story, and probably our own, instructs us that there will always be plenty of hurt and pain in life. No family business, company, or institution is immune from trouble. People do act with deliberate intent to harm others by word or deed, and it would be naive to think otherwise.

Just as Joseph acknowledged that people *did* intend to harm him, we can be frank in the same manner. This is wisdom. But in Joseph's same statement, there follows the larger truth:

> "God intended it for good, in order to preserve a numerous people, as he is doing today." (50:20–21).

At a later point, Christ, the fulfillment of all the promises to Abraham, commissioned his church as an agent of forgiveness (John 20:20–22).

The Apostle Paul amplified it by naming Christians as ambassadors of reconciliation (2 Cor. 5:18–21), even as Joseph was in his time. It is a commission that has deeply nuanced application, as we have touched on here, in our workplaces.

 *Food for Thought*

How freeing is it to know that we are commissioned as ambassadors of reconciliation, rather than judgment? Why do you think Joseph was able to push past judgment upon his brothers and offer a reconciling forgiveness?

_____

_____

_____

_____

_____

_____

_____

Joseph, the Hebrew administrator, worked for a foreign government. He saw himself as an agent of God who was instrumental in effecting the work of God with his people. From his youth, he grew wise to the harm of which people were capable, observing that sometimes people are their own worst enemies. He knew the family stories of faith mixed with doubt, of faithful service mingled with self-preservation, respect for truth but the pull into deception. He had experienced some of its consequences as he grew up—especially in the jealousies and vengeful acts of his brothers. And he experienced seven long years in a prison for a crime he hadn't committed.

Nevertheless, he valued more highly his knowledge of the promises God made to Abraham, God's amazing commitment to bless rather than judge his family, and God's wisdom in working with his people as he refined them through the fires of life. Joseph was not a person to paint over the issue of sin latent in all of us; rather, he interpreted everything he heard and experienced through his awareness of God's character and his grand work.

With faith in the steadfastness of God in fulfilling his promises, Joseph developed his administrative skill and endured years of hardship for an extraordinary reward. If we approach our own work in the same manner, it can become meaningful even in the most mundane routines, even when we are badly treated. When it is done for God, when we wait on God, we can have certainty of the day when we will hear him say, "Well done, good and faithful servant. . . . Enter into the joy of your master" (Matt. 25:21).

 Food for Thought

"Whatever you do, work heartily, as for the Lord and not for men, knowing that from the Lord you will receive the inheritance as your reward. You are serving the Lord Christ. For the wrongdoer will be paid back for the wrong he has done, and there is no partiality" (Col. 3:23–25 ESV). What new insights do you gain from this exhortation from Paul because of Joseph's story?

_____

_____

_____

_____

_____

_____

Of the many lessons about work in the book of Genesis, this one in particular endures because the pattern of Joseph's behavior points forward to humanity's ultimate deliverance from sin and death through the death and resurrection of Jesus:

> None of the rulers of this age understood this, for if they had, they would not have crucified the Lord of glory. But, as it is written,
>
> > "What no eye has seen, nor ear heard,
> >   nor the heart of man imagined,
> > what God has prepared for those who love him"—
>
> these things God has revealed to us through the Spirit. For the Spirit searches everything, even the depths of God. (1 Cor. 2:8–10 ESV)

Our places of work provide the context in which our values and character can be seen plainly, as we make decisions that affect ourselves and those around us. In his wise power, God works with our faithfulness and in our weakness. He empowers us with his own Spirit, forging hope in our hearts, even as we acknowledge our failures. And he does all this to accomplish what he himself has prepared for us who love him.

 Food for Thought

What patterns do you see in the story of Joseph that anticipate Jesus' delivery of humanity? Why is this important in regard to our work? What new respect for your own work have you gained from this study?

_____

_____

_____

_____

Prayer

Pause for a few moments of silence to reflect on this lesson. Then offer a prayer, either spontaneous or by using the following:

Lord,

Thank you for doing what Joseph couldn't do, and we cannot do: taking our sins and death upon yourself so that we can be free to live and work with you forever. Help us to count every legitimate task in this world as a contribution to the permanent world you have prepared for us.

Amen.

Conclusion: Genesis 12:1–50:21

Genesis 12–50 tells the story of the first three generations of the family through whom God chose to bring his blessings to the whole world. Having no particular power, position, wealth, fame, ability, or moral superiority of their own, they accepted his call to trust him to provide for them and fulfill the great vision he had for them.

Although God proved faithful to them in every way, their faithfulness was often fitful, timid, foolish, and precarious. They proved to be as dysfunctional as any family, yet they maintained—or at least kept returning to—the seed of faith he placed in them. Functioning in a broken world, surrounded by hostile people and powers, by faith they "invoked blessings for the future" (Heb. 11:20) and lived according to God's promises. "Therefore God is not ashamed to be called their God; indeed, he has prepared a city for them" (Heb. 11:16), the same city in which we also work as followers of "Jesus the Messiah, the son of David, the son of Abraham" (Matt. 1:1).

Key Verses and Themes from Genesis 12–50

> Now the Lord said to Abram, "Go from your country and your kindred and your father's house to the land that I will show you. I will make of you a great nation, and I will bless you, and make your name great, so that you will be a blessing. I will bless those who bless you, and the one who curses you I will curse; and in you all the families of the earth shall be blessed." So Abram went, as the Lord had told him. (12:1–4a)

God's blessing is not limited to one person's benefit. His purpose is to enable his people to be a blessing to others. Robust biblical faith is not a mere feeling; it is an active response to the divine word.

> Now Abram was very rich in livestock, in silver, and in gold. (13:2)

Wealth is not necessarily proof of God's favor or a reward for our moral behavior, but when God gives wealth we ought to consider how it may be used to bless others.

> Then Abram said to Lot, "Let there be no strife between you and me, and between your herdsmen and my herdsmen, for we are kindred. Is not the whole land before you? Separate yourself from me. If you take the left hand, then I will go to the right, or if you take the right hand, then I will go to the left." (13:8–9)

Generosity may extend beyond giving away some of our things. Giving others an active role in decision making displays our respect for them as well as our confidence in God's care for us.

> But Abram said to the king of Sodom, "I have lifted my hand to the Lord, God Most High, Possessor of heaven and earth, that I would not take a thread or a sandal strap or anything that is yours, lest you say, 'I have made Abram rich.'" (14:22–23)

In order to nullify a claim others may think they have on us, we may voluntarily relinquish what is rightfully theirs for the sake of God's purposes.

> After this, the word of the Lord came to Abram in a vision: "Do not be afraid, Abram. I am your shield, your very great reward." (15:1 NIV)

Trust in God's covenantal commitment to us is a powerful antidote to fear and uncertainty.

> [Abraham] said, "O Lord, if I have found favor in your sight, do not pass by your servant. Let a little water be brought, and wash your feet, and rest yourselves under the tree, while I bring a morsel of bread, that you may refresh yourselves, and after that you may pass on—since you have come to your servant." (18:3–5)

Although hospitality may be personally costly, it provides a context for cultivating relationships and welcomes God's presence.

> "For I [the Lord] have chosen him [Abraham], that he may charge his children and his household after him to keep the way of the Lord by doing righteousness and justice, so that the Lord may bring to Abraham what he has promised him." (18:19)

Following God's way demands a public faith whereby believers actively work for what is right, both now and for future generations.

> Abraham listened to Ephron, and Abraham weighed out for Ephron the silver that he had named in the hearing of the Hittites, four hundred shekels of silver, according to the weights current among the merchants. (23:16)

Believers may choose to honor God by doing business in a way that is contrary to the accepted custom (in this case, staged bargaining.)

> [Abraham's servant] said, "O Lord, God of my master Abraham, please grant me success today and show steadfast love to my master Abraham." (24:12)

Believers with fiduciary responsibilities serve those who commission them by depending on God's power and working for God's glory.

> But Jacob said, "I will not let you go unless you bless me." (32:26b)

In contrast to using desperate means to grasp what we want for ourselves, we recognize that God's blessings are gifts of grace to be received.

> Jacob said [to Esau], "No, please; if I find favor in your sight, then accept my present from my hand. For I have seen your face, which is like seeing the face of God, and you have accepted me." (33:10)

The work of reconciliation may be the hardest with those we are closest to, but because Christ is our peace, we can promote reconciliation around the entire world.

> Now Joseph had a dream, and when he told it to his brothers they hated him even more. (37:5)

Jealousy, envy, and false accusations are formidable obstacles, but God calls his people to patient and active trust in what God said he would do.

> His master saw that the Lord was with him and that the Lord caused all that he did to succeed in his hands. So Joseph found favor in his sight and attended him, and he made him overseer of his house and put him in charge of all that he had. (39:3–4)

> Then Pharaoh said to Joseph, "Since God has shown you all this, there is none so discerning and wise as you are. You shall be over my house, and all my people shall order themselves as you command. Only as regards the throne will I be greater than you." (41:39–40)

Knowing that God has placed believers where he wants them enables them to serve faithfully, regardless of the prominence and fame that may come with the job.

> But [Joseph] refused and said to his master's wife, "Behold, because of me my master has no concern about anything in the house, and he has put everything that he has in my charge. He is not greater in this house than I am, nor has he kept back anything from me except yourself, because you are his wife. How then could I do this great wickedness and sin against God?" (39:8–9)

The people of God are doubly accountable, working immediately for human employers and ultimately for God. But personal godliness does not necessarily guarantee that believers will always escape unjust treatment.

> Joseph answered Pharaoh, "It is not in me; God will give Pharaoh a favorable answer." (41:16)

Believers should give God credit for their skills yet be mindful of what attitudes are appropriate in the workplace where people do not share the same faith.

> "For your servant became a pledge of safety for the boy to my father, saying, 'If I do not bring him back to you, then I shall bear the blame before my father all my life.'" (44:32)

In extreme circumstances, godly leaders may need to make costly personal sacrifices in order to honor their promises and to protect the weak.

> But Joseph said to them, "Do not fear, for am I in the place of God? As for you, you meant evil against me, but God meant it for good, to bring it about that many people should be kept alive, as they are today." (50:19–20)

When forgiveness becomes a way of life, it is much easier to look beyond personal offenses and appreciate what God is doing in the long term.

> Thus he comforted them and spoke kindly to them. (50:21b)

Wisdom for Using This Study in the Workplace

Community within the workplace is a good thing and a Christian community within the workplace is even better. Sensitivity is needed, however, when we get together in the workplace (even a Christian workplace) to enjoy fellowship time together, learn what the Bible has to say about our work, and encourage one another in Jesus' name. When you meet at your place of employment, here are some guidelines to keep in mind:

- Be sensitive to your surroundings. Know your company policy about having such a group on company property. Make sure not to give the impression that this is a secret or exclusive group.

- Be sensitive to time constraints. Don't go over your allotted time. Don't be late to work! Make sure you are a good witness to the others (especially non-Christians) in your workplace by being fully committed to your work during working hours and doing all your work with excellence.

- Be sensitive to the shy or silent members of your group. Encourage everyone in the group and give them a chance to talk.

- Be sensitive to the others by being prepared. Read the Bible study material and Scripture passages and think about your answers to the questions ahead of time.

These Bible studies are based on the Theology of Work biblical commentary. Besides reading the commentary, please visit the Theology of Work website (www.theologyofwork.org) for videos, interviews, and other material on the Bible and your work.

Leader's Guide

Living Word. It is always exciting to start a new group and study. The possibilities of growth and relationship are limitless when we engage with one another and with God's word. Always remember that God's word is "alive and active, sharper than any double-edged sword" (Heb. 4:12) and when you study his word, it should change you.

A Way Has Been Made. Please know you and each person joining your study have been prayed for by people you will probably never meet but who share your faith. And remember that "the Lord himself goes before you and will be with you; he will never leave you nor forsake you. Do not be afraid; do not be discouraged" (Deut. 31:8). As a leader, you need to know that truth. Remind yourself of it throughout this study.

Pray. It is always a good idea to pray for your study and those involved weeks before you even begin. It is recommended to pray for yourself as leader, your group members, and the time you are about to spend together. It's no small thing you are about to start and the more you prepare in the Spirit, the better. Apart from Jesus, we can do nothing (John 14:5). Remain in him and "you will bear much fruit" (John 15:5). It's also a good idea to have trusted friends pray and intercede for you and your group as you work through the study.

Spiritual Battle. Like it or not, the Bible teaches that we are in the middle of a spiritual battle. The enemy would like nothing more than for this study to be ineffective. It would be part of his scheme to have group members not show up or engage in any discussion. His victory would be that your group just passes time together going through the motions of just another Bible study. You, as a leader, are a threat to the enemy as it is your desire to lead people down the path of righteousness (as taught in Proverbs). Read Ephesians 6:10–20 and put your armor on.

Scripture. Prepare before your study by reading the selected Scripture verses ahead of time.

Chapters. Each chapter contains approximately three lessons. As you work through the lessons, keep in mind the particular chapter theme in connection with the lessons. These lessons are designed so that you can go through them in thirty minutes each.

Lessons. Each lesson has teaching points with their own discussion questions. This format should keep the participants engaged with the text and one another.

Food for Thought. The questions at the end of the teaching points are there to create discussion and deepen the connection between each person and the content being addressed. You know the people in your group and should feel free to come up with your own questions or adapt the ones provided to best meet the needs of your group. Again, this would require some preparation beforehand.

Opening and Closing Prayers. Sometimes prayer prompts are given before and usually after each lesson. These are just suggestions. You know your group and the needs present, so please feel free to pray accordingly.

Bible Commentary. The Theology of Work series contains a variety of books to help you apply the Scriptures and Christian faith to your work. This Bible study is based on the *Theology of Work Bible Commentary*, examining what the Bible says about work. This commentary is intended to assist those with theological training or interest to conduct in-depth research into passages or books of Scripture.

Video Clips. The Theology of Work website (www.theologyofwork.org) provides good video footage of people from the marketplace highlighting the teaching from all the books of the Bible. It would be great to incorporate some of these videos into your teaching time.

Enjoy Your Study! Remember that God's word does not return void—ever. It produces fruit and succeeds in whatever way God has intended it to succeed.

> "So shall my word be that goes out from my mouth;
>   it shall not return to me empty,
> but it shall accomplish that which I purpose,
>   and shall succeed in the thing for which I sent it." (Isa. 55:11)

"This commentary was written exactly for those of us who aim to integrate our faith and work on a daily basis and is an excellent reminder that God hasn't called the world to go to the church, but has called the Church to go to the world."

BONNIE WURZBACHER
FORMER SENIOR VICE PRESIDENT, THE COCA-COLA COMPANY

Explore what the Bible has to say about work, book by book.

THE BIBLE AND YOUR WORK
Study Series